Fragile Heart

A Collection of Poetry by
HANNAH MOSING

Book Cover by Kristina Conatser, CapturedbyKCDesigns.com
Edited by Dragonfly De La Luz, DragonflyEditing.com
Book Design by James Woosley, FreeAgentPress.com

ISBN: 979-8-9900653-0-7 (hardcover)
ISBN: 979-8-9900653-1-4 (paperback)
ISBN: 979-8-9900653-2-1 (ebook)

Dedication

For anyone who has experienced any degree of trauma, sexual assault, or loss.

For anyone who has loved or supported someone who experienced such trauma.

For anyone who feels inescapably alone, misunderstood, or anxious…

You are not alone. These poems are for you.

symptoms of anxiety

bitten-down fingernails
constant pain roaming my body
feelings of nervousness and lack
of self-love
emotions so severe
sadness or stress feels earth-shattering
nonstop shaking and crying on the couch
happiness is so intense it makes people wonder
if you're actually ok
or why you can't stop laughing
luxury is only found in sinking
into the bed mattress
where anxiety and fatigue lie

peace

peace
is not just
a feeling
but
a state
of being

peace
begins deep
in your core
it cannot be
cultivated
all at once
no,
peace
grows naturally

peace
is my
safety net
peace
provides
comfort

peace
is a hug
that
you receive
when you
are physically
mentally
and emotionally
alone

peace is
beautiful,
peace is tranquil,
peace is where I want to live

eyes

you can tell a lot about a person by their eyes
based on how they look
or what they've seen
most eyes are tired or worried
in the mirror,
what do your eyes tell you?
you try to convince others
that you're happy by smiling
through the pain
but your irises can't lie
neither can the bags that weigh heavy
on your lovely face
eyes are like windows
you can make the curtains around them
look pretty
you could even clean them up a bit
but you can't hide the windows to your soul

in the middle

I am the second child of three, the middle child
naturally the mediator
for all conflicts and issues
even in my list of priorities,
I placed myself
second to last
not first,
because there were other people's problems
to attend to
not last
but in the middle
I have been placed in the middle of things,
good and bad
being a middle child has its perks
and its pitfalls
the oldest child is pressured with setting expectations
the youngest is spoiled and coddled,
especially my autistic brother
but the middle child is the caretaker,
the peacemaker of the family
me, the middle child of three

pretzel crisps

as silly as it sounds
I find myself coping
by eating pretzel crisps
when I was a child
I would eat them in such an intricate way
a pretzel between my two little fingers
I would nibble along the edges
so as not to break
the pretzel's twisted form
but if I chewed too hard
and broke it
I would shove the pretzel in my mouth
out of pure frustration
each grain of salt met my teeth
one at a time
then the pretzel edges
when I had made it all the way around
only then would I be satisfied

isn't it strange how children cope
when they can't cry in the backseat
they just eat the pretzels mommy gave them
in silence,
gnawing their way to the end of the twist
for the entire car ride
until there's nothing left
but the remnants
of saltiness and dryness
the same kind you feel on the inside
is the taste of pretzels on the outside –
salty, dry
rough around the edges
an odd but sad metaphor
my inner child, coping

unplanned planner

I go by many things
but mostly
a planner
I love lists
being organized
keeping it together
yet everything
in my life
seems unplanned
and I've never been good
at keeping things together
Like when my parents stopped
loving each other
I struggled
to find out why
but later learned
how sorry I would be
to know
there are only so many things
you can learn
to keep track of
or anticipate

you can make a list and
expect to get things done
you could go so far
as to plan for it
but life is unplanned
still I like to try
my pen and my paper
my notes on my phone
planning things

cigarette

whenever I smell a cigarette,
I'm instantly reminded
of how things used to be
no one smokes because they want to
just because they have to
nicotine, the body's enemy
my family smoked
to cope but I knew
at a very young age
that nicotine was not for me
I'd sneak into the backyard
where adults hid their cancer
sticks, fold them inside a paper towel
and throw it away
little did I know
that was only one box
out of twenty-five
yes, I counted
I wasn't stupid

even if it's taken hold of my family
it will never touch my lips
the smoke
will never fill my lungs
the tar
will never kill me
why would I smoke to cope
when I can step outside
and fill my lungs with Nature's embrace?
the air that keeps me breathing
that turns breath into life
not the smoke that takes it

shadow

I am a shadow
craving to be in your path
a distant outline

bluebirds

when my nana passed, I saw a bluebird
hues of indigo, sky blue, and white
amongst its feathers
every time I looked outside,
bluebirds flying gracefully
in her luscious, green backyard
I wondered
then I realized
it was her
disguised as an angel
a symbol of joy and love
watching over me
until it's my time
to join her in the skies

work

long hours spent sitting and working
feels dull and strenuous
but when 5 o'clock hits
I spring up from my desk
power-walk out of my office, down the stairs
into the evening sun
the air warming my cold body
with each step, I take in fresh air
my gaze shifts to the people
trickling out of buildings
finding their way to their fixed destination
I walk for several minutes
until my feet pull me into the parking garage
where I guess I parked my car
ride up the elevator
as my hand finds the car handle
and my body hits the seat
I know I'm headed home until tomorrow

music

when I listen to music,
I'm transported
far away from here
to a feeling of serenity
music
tells us stories
sounds that intrigue
lyrics that transform
bringing your mind,
body,
and soul
together as one
my love
for music
is as strong as the breeze
that flows through my hair
on my morning walk
when it's just me,
myself,
and music

exes

what's worse…
an ex-lover
or an ex-friend?

on one hand,
you could say

an ex-lover is worse
someone who knew you
to your core
who promised you forever
then left you there with never

on the other hand,
I would argue

an ex-friend
stings just a little harder
sometimes much harder
than even losing your first love ever did
friends can evolve
into family for life
or at least
they're supposed to
what I wasn't warned about
was how volatile the process can be

you can block an ex-lover
and never see their face again
but an ex-friend
can be so intricately
intermingled with your social life
that it's harder to delete them

you go from late-night talking
every other day
to hollow exchanges
from the warmest interactions
to a demeanor so cold
it sends a chill down your spine
or words so scalding
they sizzle through your gooey core
like acid
what was once a spirited exchange
quietly translated
into a look
that speaks louder than words
a cold-blooded stare
that pierces your heart
and jumbles your brain

'til nothing makes sense
and you're alone again…

afraid

what am I afraid of?

I'm afraid of wasps
scorpions
anything
that can sting

that's me being polite

what am I really afraid of?
myself
I'm afraid
that I'm not kind
I'm afraid
that I hurt
the ones I love

like a scorpion,
with an invisible stinger
sending pain piercing
through your body

I'm afraid
of the things
that are impolite
to bring up in public
myself, I'm afraid of myself
I'm afraid
of others
I'm afraid
of living
I'm afraid…

skeletons in the closet

I have skeletons
in the closet
everyone does
mine have collected
dust over the years
they're still
in there
waiting
watching
wanting
for me to cave in
please, let us see
the light of day
they whisper
we won't hurt you,
we promise
as they lie between
their bony teeth

I open the door
but my hands
will me not to
give in, not to
reach for them
the temptation
is there, but
I refuse
my skeletons
are in the closet
for a reason

censored

WARNING:
this content is rated R
rated A for Assault
P for Pornographic
E for Every time this happens,
it's censored
a black bar hovering over my body parts
I only wish it would cover the secrets of my heart
I'm censored, my senses
overloaded
sensory movements tingle
a burning sensation
I'm bleeding and feeling
and it's too much
can't you see the damage you've done?

WARNING:
the person you're about to violate
doesn't see it coming
you had to go and touch me
where I didn't want it
you just couldn't resist
it wasn't enough
that you had to cum in through the front
and back doors, no,
you just sat on the couch
in my home
that once housed my comfort
designed to make me feel less alone
but then you mowed over my boundaries
and watched the uncensored version
until your eyes went dry
unwanted hands
caressing my thighs

I am censored
this body is not for your viewing pleasure
so kindly change the channel
don't look
and
don't
touch

adrenaline

blood pumping
heart pounding
body moving
mind racing
adrenaline rush

the storm

your life
entwined
with mine
was like the calm
before the storm
we both saw it brewing
on the horizon
just a matter of where
and when
the storm
took shape
in small doses

but
the rain would
pour
over me endlessly
for another three years
after
your constant,
unwanted
attention
drenched me
in acid rain
I felt each raindrop
consistently
you hurt me
through the self-inflicted cuts
on my wrists
no protection
from the umbrella

Fragile Heart

I covered myself with
your existence
seeping through
the worn-out fabric
no escaping
your toxicity
even when I thought
it could get better
if I just
packed up and left
you found a way
to torment me
for another three years
soaking me to the bone
so deep no sun
could ever pierce
through to dry me

scream

why do I scream at you?
say things I don't mean
because I want to disappear?
or my heart remains unseen...

bromeliad

bromeliad
a symbol of protection
shield of beauty

would you rather

when I was in middle school
I would play
"would you rather"
with my friends
at first, the questions were simple
would you rather
have hands for feet?
or feet for hands?
but suddenly
the game wasn't simple anymore
the questions got harder
in high school
would you rather
give a handjob or a blowjob?
I would rather
do none of the above
you know what I would rather?

I would rather have not been raped
at only twenty-two
I would rather
be anywhere than here
I would rather
move apartments than to stay
in that bedroom any longer
I would rather have suffered silently
than to hear my screams
bouncing off the walls
I would rather
have a healthy breakup
than one that ended
in lies and accusations
you weren't assaulted,

you cheated on me
you thought I did it for pleasure
the person that did this is an ASSaulter
I'd rather the toxic men in my life
SHUT THE FUCK UP
and make their ears bleed
from hearing what I have to say
I would rather have feet for hands
so I would look like such a monstrosity
that no one would touch me
but it doesn't matter
what I would rather
the only real question is
"what would you prefer to happen first?"
would you rather be kissed
then get brutally fucked after?
or would you rather not have eyes
so you can't see what's happening?
would you rather be alive
or feel like the only way out is to die?
what would you rather?

oblivion

humans, in a constant state of oblivion
unaware
ignorant
careless

some unintentionally oblivious
walking down the street
eyes on their phone
the bright, white screen
draws them in so deeply
completely unaware
of what's walking
in their path
separate existences
now colliding

others are more purposeful
with their oblivion
claiming to be forgetful
when, in fact,
they choose
what they want to remember
it's easier
to be oblivious
than ignorant
for seeing the suffering
and still doing nothing

water

when I was younger
I dreamt I could turn
into a mermaid
creature of the sea
friend to all
magical beyond being
keeper of that
which keeps us alive
quenches the thirst
of all living things

wash, rinse, repeat

wash,
rinse,
repeat

wash away the tears
that streak down your lovely face
rinse the pain,
both physical and emotional
repeat until dry
or until you can no longer cry

wash,
rinse,
repeat

wash your delicate skin
where he touched you
until your skin practically falls off
rinse yourself from head to toe
repeat until the well runs dry
until there is no more water
to wash your tarnished body with

wash,
rinse,
repeat

wash away the memories
rinse off his stinging words
repeat until you no longer
feel shame for a crime
you didn't commit

wash,
rinse,
repeat

wash,
rinse,
repeat

wash,

rinse,

repeat

aftermath of assault

cold
dark
wet
painful
jarring
lonely
lost
this is
the aftermath
of assault

decay

my skin is breaking
parts of me fading
slowly
death has taken hold

Hannah Mosing

sometimes I wonder

sometimes I wonder
if you ever really miss me
I no longer miss you
I miss the person
that you used to be

darkness

darkness envelops me
it wraps around my body slowly
like a snake wrapping itself around its prey
squeezing every ounce of life out
until its eyes close
its heartbeat slows
and then
it becomes still
for the darkness is no longer hungry
its appetite has been satisfied
by the ones that surrender to its hold

enigma

understanding you
forever will be difficult
you are an enigma
puzzling
mysterious
a riddle
that doesn't want to be solved

tell me why

tell me why my rapist
gets to live a normal life
while I carry this burden in my body
slowly feeling less alive
tell me why my rapist
did what he did
why he touched me
and fucked me
until I bled
tell me why
I'm still living traumatized
reliving every sensation
from the terrifying thoughts in this brain
to the intense penetration between these legs
tell me why I screamed and cried and
no one came
no one cared
if I lived or died
I felt it all and nothing
at the same time, desensitized

I looked at myself from the outside in
watched myself drown,
lost the strength to swim
a part of me died that day
the day my life changed
I couldn't do anything to stop it
the damage was already done
I was raped in the bathroom, shower,
in my bed
when he left I lost it
I cried
until the tears
dried
tell me why I was assaulted
by someone I trusted
because not knowing is a knife
twisting and mangling me inside

flames

pain engulfs my heart
in flames
my soul is burning
constantly crying
begging
for someone to extinguish
the fire
the pain
in my body is unbearable
it feels like
I'm dying
yet I'm still here
wondering when the flames
will go out
wondering if the pain
will subside
the fire in my mind will burn
until I can't handle
the heat

until I'm reduced to nothing
but ashes
the flames
feel like a thousand claws
tearing and tarnishing
this body that smolders
with anxiety
this fire
will never protect me from cold
instead it tortures me
until I can't withstand it anymore
my own personal hell
that no one knows
the screams
turn into lullabies
my demons of trauma
leave me desensitized
no amount of water
or medication can put out
the fire
because my soul has already been burned alive

letter to the ones I've lost

this is a letter
to the loved ones I've lost
physically, mentally
spiritually, emotionally
I know you are always with me
but your physical entity is not
and for that, I mourn

to encapsulate my emotions,
the tears my tired eyes cry,
I write you a letter
in hopes that you read it
and make your spiritual being
felt and known to my
fragile heart:

Dear Beloved Lost,

I think about you every day
that you are not here
on this vast and lonely Earth
with me.
I reach for my phone
to call you…
You would always
answer me….
Do you still wonder how I'm doing?
Are you proud of me?
Hello?
Are you there?
It's ok if you don't respond.
I know that your soul is
occupied with moving on.

But I hope you know
how much I miss you,
how I long for your hugs
that soaked up my tears,
instantly lifting the heavy weight
of anxiety that resides within
You made me feel whole.
Seen.
Loved.
I hope I made you feel the same.

When you were physically here with me,
you always loved me,
even when I acted cruelly.
I hope you know that I am sorry
for every mean word I ever said.
Know that it was not from me,
but from a darker self
I'm still trying to escape.

I hope you know that you are missed.
We think of you every day,
how you cherished all the time spent
with your family and friends.
It's hot in Texas, but we still
plant you flowers.
I think that's when I feel
your spirit the most.

I hope I get to see you again,
in another world,
another life,
in an afterlife
of your hugs,
your love,
and your beautiful,
happy soul.

Love eternally,
Hannah

January

the beginning of a new year
transition from Christmas to New Year's Eve
feeling anything but ordinary, January
a fresh start, something better to come, or so I'm told

new year, same routine
back to school, work meetings,
a time for reminiscing
past memories, future endeavors, wanting to feel seen

early mornings drinking tea in bed
stepping outside for a walk in the crisp winter air
waking up to see the sun rising above your head
and saying a silent prayer

let this be my year
let this year be good
let me feel warmth, not fear
let me be happy, as I rightfully should.

Hannah Mosing

raindrops

raindrops
pitter-patter
on my window
each drop
delicately formed
how beautiful it is
to see the sky
crying
whether she is weeping
tears of anger
sobbing and wailing
emphasized
by low guttural claps
of thunder
or tears of joy
in pure appreciation
for the ground below her
slow, steady tears fall

drip
drop
drip
drop

the sky we dream under
releases the loveliest tears
I wish my tears
were as lovely as hers

nightmares

my trauma likes to visit when I sleep
I wake up drenched in sweat
most of my dreams lately
turn out to be nightmares
taunting me through snapshots of the past
me, looking at myself
watching my body get violated
over and over again
tears rolling down my face
my soul screaming under water
no one could hear me while I drowned

translucent

you are translucent
I see right through your facade
a transparent fool

isn't it crazy?

isn't it crazy
that I haven't spoken
to you in years
yet I remember
our last conversation
like it was yesterday?

isn't it crazy
that we were together
for four years
yet in that time
I never truly knew you?

isn't it crazy
that I helped you grieve
the loss of someone close to you
but when I lost the person
closest to me
you barely gave me sympathy?

even though I held you in your grief
every night until you fell asleep crying?

isn't it crazy
that when I was assaulted
you told our friends
I cheated on you
so you could justify
breaking my heart
even though you knew how fragile it was?

isn't it crazy
that I once idolized you
my partner in crime
yet now when I dream of you
I despise your existence
even in my subconscious
far more than I ever admired you?

I know, right?
isn't it fucking crazy?

Hannah Mosing

bones of glass, heart of gold

my bones may be glass
but my heart is made of gold
the purest kind
a value that has no number
heart in my chest
housed by aching bones
the kind that ache over time
but have a steadfast foundation
to hold this gleaming heart

for anyone who tries
to tarnish the gold
to shatter my bones
or my delicate being

good luck

I have bones of glass

and a heart of fucking gold

I remain intact

I'm still standing

a letter to my rapist

how do I start?
I can't bear to speak your name
let alone write it
"dear asshole" sounds fitting, so…

dear asshole,

how dare you?
how dare you try to ruin my life?
how
dare
you…

I hope you feel ashamed
I hope you feel my pain
I hope you lie in bed at night
hating yourself
a little more
than the day before

I hope
you rot
in hell

that's what I really want to say
except I'm "too nice"
to those who never deserved
my friendship in the first place

but if our paths somehow cross again
(fuck, I hope they never do)
this is what I'll say to you:

"hey asshole"

wait, no
that sounds too formal

you don't deserve a greeting
that addresses you by name
or even by insult
leaves a sour taste in my mouth
all too familiar because of you
fuck a greeting
I will just go straight in
like you did to me
I will look you in the eye
unflinching this time
my voice will be heard
and you will obey my command:

don't come near me
don't touch me
with hands nor eyes

Fragile Heart

it is too much
for me to bear
physically and mentally
I have deteriorated
do you even understand
the damage you've done?
no, apparently you don't
but I will see to it
that you understand completely
I, too, can give you no other choice

because you were the one
that spiked my drink
you were the one
that made me want to stop
being alive

I hope you live with that burden
for the rest of your life
as I now have to
as my relationship now has to
if it can even survive this…

do you even know
how many people got hurt
because you broke me
knowing full well
I was in a relationship
with someone you professed to respect?

finally, and in spite of you,
I am healthier now
I am safe
I am happy
with a new love
a new life
without you in it
so go right ahead
propose to her
you fucking psychopath

just do me a favor
(you owe me this much, at least)
and stay
the fuck
away
from me
that's the only "forever" I need anymore

Hannah Mosing

new beginning

flowers are blooming
a new beginning
spring is upon us

breaking point

all living things
have a breaking point
for wildflowers, it's when their roots
become eradicated
daisies torn out of the ground
by the small, grubby hands
of the third-grade bully
that just so happens to like you
except he doesn't just like you…
he "likes you" likes you
normally, it would make you feel giddy
but deep down you know
it's no innocent crush
what he feels for you
is obsession
when you want infatuation
or at the very least
a bit of admiration
or human decency would be nice

instead, he pulls the delicate flowers
out from the soil
with unnecessary force
until the grass surrounding the flower
is uprooted as well
he shoves the broken daisies
into your hands
smiling with a look of pure and raw
obsession
looking at you proudly and claiming,
"I picked these for you"
but you know deep down
why he picked them
he may have "picked" those daisies for you
but by taking the ground's children
away from their mother
he caused dreaded feelings
of uneasiness

Fragile Heart

tears fall down your face,
bouncing off the leaves
why would he give you life
in the form of death
flowers ripped away
from Mother Nature's hands
his unwanted advances make you want to
rip off your skin
until you're nothing
bones and rubble
as he puts his hands where he shouldn't
you feel the petals on your shoulders,
your legs
your thighs

soon, you will become a daisy
who tries day after day
to stay rooted in Mother Earth
using what little nutrients are left in its stem
in an attempt to revive itself
but once a flower gets pulled from its home
the flower dries out
until the petals crumble
one by one
the daisy is no longer a flower
the remnants of what used to be an untouched garden
now the blueprint for the next breaking point

instincts

humans are taught
to trust their instincts
follow their gut
but how can I
hear my instincts
between the loud sobs
from my heart
and the angry yells
from my mind?

my brain and heart
constantly at war
deciphering between
right and wrong

I feel like
my instincts
hurt me
work against me
cruelly
sadistically

Hannah Mosing

falling

everyone talks about
falling in love

but falling out of love
is a much longer fall

down a black abyss
of loneliness

when I first fell in love
I lost my footing
falling for someone
who hid behind a mask
pretended to love me
declared himself
my soulmate
while I fell
thinking I'd have
the soft, green grass
to catch me

with your hand in mine
you said we'd be fine
you lied
but I fell
then tears fell
down my pale
tired face

when you pushed me off the edge
I grabbed for your hand
still open and extended
you clutched it
then laughed
releasing your grip
I counted on you
to hold my hand
or at least warn me
about the impact
of falling out of love
and landing in darkness

when my body broke
against the ground
I struggled to move
the wind knocked out of me
as I began to stand,
I felt where the rock collided
with my delicate skin
sun burning my ivory legs
reminding me
that I'm alive
I survived
the chaos
stunned but determined
and found beauty
shattered
broken
beauty

Fragile Heart

I willed my body
to get up
to show him
that despite falling
crashing
fracturing
I could and I would
stand up again
I'd dust myself off
wash away the blood
dirt
and tears

even after you,
I still fell
repeatedly, eventually
falling hurt
a little less
until one day
falling felt like flying
hand in hand
with someone who saved me
from falling
into darkness
and helped me
to fall in light
into happiness
into love
with him

in light
into happiness
into love
with myself
in light
into happiness
in love

aggression

aggression rushes over me like a tidal wave
slow at first then all at once
crashing into my core, hijacking my mind
until words fly out
sharper than knives
the victim of my verbal damage cries
tears of blood
I've hurt them from the inside out
their heart is bludgeoned
begging me to stop
but I cannot contain my rage
those that hurt me
hurt me so deeply
that madness takes over
the blood on my hands
is my own
victim of my own aggression
maybe my tears someday
will be normal, salty tears
not floods of red liquid erupting from my bloodshot eyes

whisper

why is it that
when I scream
no one can hear me
but when I whisper
my quiet pleas are deafening?

Hannah Mosing

tears

water flowing fast
tears rushing from her eyelids
her sad heart cries

hug

a lot can be said through a hug
when you're falling apart
and your shoulders shake
so hard it makes
trees tremble
when words aren't enough
a hug
makes it better
a hug you can feel
more than words you ever will

Hannah Mosing

Ode to Evelyn

I miss you
every single hour of every single day
spiritually, you're with me
physically, we're apart
I wish the pain of losing you
would go away
but the emptiness I feel
still remains in my heart

I dream of you at night
think of you in the morning
I call to tell you all about it,
but God answers the call
and listens
He knows
my sorrows, how hard I cried in my mourning
He reminds me
that you're an angel now
a star in the sky that glistens

Fragile Heart

Evelyn, my grandmother,
a woman I hold so dear
more than a mother and grandparent
you were my beloved friend
you had nothing to fear
courageous until the very end

Granny, I love you
however far, however near
with every breath and every tear
I will see you again.

Hannah Mosing

fragile heart

be careful with my heart
for it is fragile
shards of my past
placed back together
shattered
reconstructed
again and again
a never-ending cycle

but that's life, isn't it?

fragile is my heart
and tired
please have patience
for she is delicate
her core made of
colorful pieces
once pristine
now jagged

Fragile Heart

all I ask
is please be gentle
one wrong move
and my heart will shatter
all over again
then it will be
nothing but pieces
then I'll be standing
barefoot, bleeding, broken
picking up and putting back together
again

Hannah Mosing

color

in my formerly
dark
opaque
existence
in this world so full of gray
you are a splash of color
you are the reason I stay

sunshine

to me, you are like sunshine
warm on my skin, brighter than life
takes more than a storm to dull your light
my personal sunshine
at my lowest, you lift me up
at my best, you lift me higher
your warmth seeps through me
like a rainbow
emerging from the clouds on a dreary day
my sunshine
the brightest love I have ever known

validation

I needed validation

when no one else believed

you

make

me

feel

seen

sore throat

are you ok? you sound like you have a sore throat
I'm ok. It's probably just allergies…

I know all too well why my throat hurts
yes, the brutal Texas weather is one factor
the nightmare from the night before is another…
but that's not what this is
I know what this is
it's me
my throat is sore because of
me
crying and screaming the night before
hurting the person I love through vile and
untrue words
saying things mid-panic attack
I know I don't mean

WE'RE DONE!
SHUT THE FUCK UP!
I CAN'T THINK STRAIGHT!

followed by
I love you
I'm sorry
you deserve better

why is my brain at war with itself?
why did I scream so loudly
when all I had to do was open my mouth
and tell him I have no control
over these intrusive thoughts?
then I'd be heard, not hurt
seen, not mean
to the person I love
and wants nothing but the best
for me

I was screaming at my inner demons
I didn't want to scream at him
or ignore the friend that called at 1 a.m.
to check on me
no, it was the demons
clawing their way out, scratching open my organs
creating their version of mental purgatory
just for me
until there's nothing left but shreds
of the person I used to be
the kind, bubbly, sunshine-filled girl that Granny would see
before she passed away
and the world turned gray

people say trauma helps shape you
my trauma likes to torture me instead
it's only when I remember to breathe
swallow my tears
cry until it hurts
a little less
that I can find sunshine again
after all,
you can't have a rainbow
without a little rain
or in my case, a downpour
to drown the demons
keep the sad thoughts away

even after a hurricane, the sun finds its home
in the sky and onto my cold shoulders
warming me up
until I feel whole
until I fill the hole
in my heart from the storm
my body endures

compare and contrast

when you look up at the trees,
what do you see?
do you see the birds
and the butterflies
dancing amongst the leaves?

or do you see rays of sun
poking through the branches
as heat beams down, forming
beads of sweat across your head

all of a sudden, you feel
a sense of dread
not appreciation for
this beautiful world
we live in, but instead
frustration for not
taking the time to
"stop and smell the roses"

there are days when
all I can see is beauty
but sometimes
my surroundings feel
claustrophobic

when this happens,
I try to compare and contrast
myself in relation to
what's around me

compare and contrast
the sunlit trees
to your delicate hands

compare and contrast
the vast complexity
of this world we live in
to the simplicity that
nature and all things
in it can bring forth

compare and contrast
the anxiety in your body
to the present moment

compare and contrast
your breath to the
sounds of the wind
singing praises of joy

breathe in, breathe out
and you will be okay
and hopefully find a way
to the beauty in the chaos

compare and contrast
but let go of your past
and see what the future
has in store for you

depression

your sadness pierces through me
like a knife in my heart
constantly stabbing me in the back

the body

they say the body is a temple
a wonderland
a garden to be tended
this body I was given
is a rugged terrain
filled with wildflowers
and crisp, springtime wind
made up of trees rooted
in decades-old soil
that stand firm despite the storms
they have weathered
the body is made up of bones
water
life
each inhale the body takes
releases an even greater exhale
with each breath,
the body expresses gratitude
on hard days, the body is simply grateful
to still be standing

on easy days, the body exists peacefully
and on days where the body's spirit struggles
it wills itself to move,
to take a step forward,
to fight
your body is a treasure to behold
unique body, mind, and soul
tailored to you and only you
treat it kindly
nourish it and cherish it
for you never know which day
your body breathes its last

autumn leaves

autumn leaves
rustle and crack
under my shoes
as I run home
to you
you take me in
to your loving embrace
the smell of autumn
hangs in the air
like pine cones
hanging from
a tall forest tree
oh, how I love
the season of fall
embracing the
changes of nature
the beauty of it all

stinging

my eyes
were constantly stinging
when you were around
red
puffy
sad
how could my eyes feel so dry
when the tears came like ocean waves
rushing in
slowly receding
then washing back to shore again

fighting back tears
that's when my eyes
sting the most
it's the pull from my heartstrings
through my eye sockets
into my brain
that reasons you should love me
and not judge me

but you told me things that were
more hurtful than helpful
cut me off at the knees
in my already crippling anxiety

calm down
stop crying
you're crazy!
what's wrong with you?

what's wrong is it was you
who promised to make my heart sing
but only made my eyes sting
what's wrong is it was you
who never truly loved me

I hope one day you know the sting
the deepest cuts of judgment bring
I hope they leave you pale and flaccid
I hope they burn your eyes like acid
disintegrate your tear ducts
destroy your irises
until the only thing your eyes can see
is your callous criticism of me

snow flurries

I don't like the cold,
but I love catching
snow flurries
with you
laughing, shivering
our tongues stuck out
awaiting the falling
precipitation from the crisp
Colorado air
bringing forth a feeling
of pure bliss
that I would choose to have
over anything else
any day

grief

let me tell you something about grief
because I have felt it
on more than one occasion
not just in the form of death

I have grieved life itself

grief is inevitable

at one point or another,
you will experience grief
whether you lose someone
or your sanity
you will feel it
trust me, you will

grief is forever

people say it gets easier
that every day that passes
you're a little less sad
but every day you will feel it
every day you are here
and every day after
your soul leaves this planet

grief is relentless

grief will strike at all hours
when you're trying to sleep
while you're at work for ten hours straight
even in your happiest moments
you will feel it
you will feel empty
you will feel their absence
you will feel it
all the fucking time

grief is a teacher

a difficult teacher
since nothing in life is easy
grief will teach you
how to cope
and live your life
to the fullest
grief teaches us
to appreciate
the people we love
grief teaches us
that we are human
we will all experience it
we must all embrace it
even if we don't want to

grief is real

whatever deity you believe in
or don't
grief is real
and felt from the heart
grief is a shirt
with the tag facing out
inside exposed
for all to see

grief is normal

I have grieved
over myself
my state of being
my immense lows
I continue to grieve
my grandmother, Evelyn
I still try to
call her or text her sometimes
grief
is felt when there is change
and you never know
who's masking their grief
behind a smiling face

grief is *inevitable*
grief is *forever*
grief is *relentless*
grief is a *teacher*
grief is *real*
grief
     is
        normal

Hannah Mosing

when we're together

when we're together
time stops
I look at you,
your brown eyes closed,
resting from the day

your head rests on my chest
and my fragile heart rests
in your loving hands

remember when

remember when
I used to see you
after school
and do my homework
you made homemade
shrimp and crab legs
with an ice cold glass
of Coca-Cola
how we'd stay up late
to watch the same
movie or two
before we fell asleep

I remember when
you got sick
when you couldn't
cook your own food
how your body
grew tired, still
it woke up
and fought through
another day

remember when
you decorated and
dressed up
in extravagant costumes
every Halloween
and threw a party
for the whole neighborhood

I remember when
I would help you
put on your costume
because even after
you were diagnosed
with cancer
you were determined
to dress up
even if only
for a few minutes
before getting
back into bed

remember when
you were told
that the cancer
could not be
removed
that it had spread
too much
and all any of us could do
was wait

I remember when
you passed away
I had just seen you
a few days before
but I didn't know
that it would be
the last time
I would hug you
or tell you
I love you

remember when
I used to tell you
that you were
the best granny
anyone could ever have

I remember when
it was time
to lay you to rest
I didn't want to
accept that you were gone
from this Earth
you had told me
you didn't want to die
and you were scared

I remember when
we were all scared

but hopeful

I remember when
you fought until
the very end
how strong you were
how grateful I was
to have you
even just a little longer
selfishly

I remember when

you were alive

I remember when

you died

I remember when

Hannah Mosing

cherry blossoms

pink cherry blossoms
a sign of renewal
the start of springtime

loving you

I love loving you
your head rests on my shoulder
I know I am home

craving

I crave you
the taste of you
on my lips…

burnt bridges

if I burnt bridges
would you call me an arsonist?
what if I did it
for my own protection?
whose side would you take?
what side of the bridge
would you stand on?

for me, there is no side
I'm stuck in the middle
if I burn it, I am relieved of pain
but more likely to fall
into the empty pit below
if I try to cross it
or improve its structure
I risk losing
my authenticity
I risk falling
from a bridge
that is more likely to break
under its own weight
than dissipate into ashes

to protect myself
I burn bridges
to protect those I love
I burn bridges
I burn bridges

a letter to myself

Dear Hannah,

You are too kind
to others
when you should be careful
who you grant kindness to.
You are too forgiving of those
who continue to hurt you.
Do me — yourself — a favor.
And stop.

Stop making other people's
happiness your priority.
Start making yours
a priority instead.
Stop blaming yourself for things
that are the fault of others
even if it feels like the fault is yours.

Your mind can be your biggest enemy,
but it can also be your friend.
Spend more time
in self-reflection,
because you only have this one
precious life to live.
Spend more time
doing what makes you happy.
Spend more time
with those who bring a smile to your face,
not more tears.

You are beautiful.
You are worthy.
You are a force
to be reckoned with.
Act like it.

Have courage amidst self-doubt.
Have faith
in yourself.
You can do so much,
but only if you allow yourself
to live
for yourself.

When you feel anxious,
like your world
is in shambles,
remember to breathe.
Inhale, letting your anxieties be felt
to the maximum point.
Exhale, letting those anxieties go out of your body,

Oh, Hannah, I want you to know
that no matter how isolating
anxiety
PTSD
depression
et cetera
can feel for you,
you are NEVER alone.
Especially when you feel
like giving up
is the only option,
that is when to push forward
the hardest, because there are
people who would miss you
if you were gone.

Don't give up.
Ever.

I am here for you.
Always.

Love yourself.

Love,
Your Self

the bookshelf

my life can be explained by a bookshelf
a simple but timeless antique
each shelf tells a story
colorful trinkets spark nostalgic memories
encompassing my feelings and overall perspective on life
the top shelf lined with teddy bears
and cheesy sign quotes
reminding me to "live life"
and say "I love you to the moon and back"
which makes me smile and think of my mother
the second and third shelves tell the story
of my love for photos, music, and Batman
the last two shelves —
ironically enough, the only ones with books —
childhood stories of adventure and suspense
the bookshelf representing me
from the ground up

divine

she is so divine
a sight to breathe in
as much as behold

desire

I yearn
for your touch
slow,
passionate
exhaling
my desire
for you

gaslighter

my flames
are ignited with rage
you cannot turn my soul
into ashes
you might light
my fuel
my body may be tainted
by your destructive hand
but your gaslighting
will never
burn away my soul

embrace yourself

embrace
who you are
not how others
perceive you
give love
to yourself

home

a house is not a home
without love and comfort
a place where you feel seen and understood
a refuge meant to keep your demons at bay
so you may feel peace
at the end of the day
a house is just a structure
that keeps you safe
nothing more than bricks, wood,
and other little things
but a home is your way of living
your way of creating
balance in your surroundings
a home is meant to house all feelings
to feel at home
is a warm welcome
when you have nowhere else to go,
when you miss his hugs
that feel like home

Hannah Mosing

when you're stressed
and need somewhere to get
a sense of relief
a home does not only constitute
the physical building
a home is a feeling
unlike any other
the space that keeps you content
when your energy is spent
come back home
and feel safe again
even if only in nature
satiated by your surroundings
birds in the skies
to keep you company
fireflies at night
to light the way
shimmering oh so beautifully
in the evening sky
this is what home is
if you are without shelter,
come to me
my door is always open

mountains

my heart belongs to the mountains
crisp air dancing with snow flurries
surrounded by a plethora of trees
sunrise and sunset so stunning
it makes your eyes water
walking through the town of Breckenridge
watching the skies as day turns to night
stars sprinkled throughout the canvas
of Mother Earth's design
I feel it in my bones
my heart belongs to the mountains
and that is where I must go

pink sky

my favorite time of day
is when the sun sets
and Mother Earth starts to rest
hues of pink, purple, and blue
dance amongst the trees
and the never-ending clouds in the sky
colors so beautiful
it makes me want to cry
tears of joy
for I am so grateful
to call the pink sky
my home away from home

fighting sleep

I am fighting sleep
just to look into your eyes
you're my favorite dream

parallel universe

what would happen
if we lived this lifetime
in a parallel universe?

would we have met?
what if we hadn't?

in a parallel universe,
I could lose
the origin of myself
my brain would be
too focused on
multiple realities
that could take place

what if I lost you, too?

my life could be
quite different
for better or for worse
and just maybe I could live in a reality
where I didn't feel pain,
sadness, or grief

but then
I wouldn't really
be living,
would I?

some like to imagine
that in another universe,
they would live a
more fulfilled life
but I say you can have it right here
because our universe is made up
of good and bad
and no matter how heavy
your burdens feel,
everything happens for a reason

the only parallel reality
I would want to exist in
is the one
that I currently live in
appreciating the good
persevering through the bad
embracing it all
enjoying my youth

roller coaster

loving someone
is like a roller coaster
that never stops

the coaster represents love
the tracks symbolize
this path of life
we ride together

am I scared
when we get to the top?
yes.
I anticipate the drop,
scared of what feeling
it may bring

will I feel the thrill
of how well you love me
or get scared and
scream for the ride to stop?
fearful that I am too timid
to be loved so deeply

feeling the wind
through my hair
the pause
at the top of the ride
is the scariest of all

but then I look at you
and know I am safe
that no matter what feelings
this ride evokes
I will feel it
with you by my side

Fragile Heart

the "whoosh" felt
after we descend together
makes us erupt
in laughter
the jolts and turns
as I stop holding on
and learn to let go
of my insecurity

over and over
we ride this roller coaster
I hope it never stops

soulmate

you are the **S**unlight in my life
the **O**nly one I want to be with
you are **U**ndeniably wonderful
thank you for **L**oving all of me
you are **M**y other half
and you're **A**lways there for me
Tender in how you kiss me,
hug me, love me
I hope I get to spend **E**ternity
with you by my side

what you mean to me

I want to tell you
exactly
what you mean to me
what you are
what you represent
your importance
and remind you
of your significance
to myself
and others

you are honey
sweet
pure
golden
honey

Hannah Mosing

you are the sky
endless
abundant
strikingly
breathtaking
to gaze upon

you are vivacious
effervescent,
full of life

you mean the world to me
because you are the world to me

comfort

there is no one else
that brings me comfort
like you do
feeling your head
on my chest
rise and fall
of our breath
aligned with one another

you bring me comfort
with you I feel safe
no one else knows how
to console my heart
except for you

I write this as you sleep
peacefully next to me
so that I never lose this
cozy feeling of quiet contentment
between us

the smell of your hair
makes me deliriously happy
the feeling of you in my arms
is so surreal
sometimes I wait
for the Universe to pinch me
to tell me that it's all been a dream

I dreamed of this feeling for so long
to trust another person
with my entire being
two souls breathing as one

if I really am dreaming
I don't want to wake up
unless it's next to you
unless it's next to you...

About the Author

Hannah is a survivor on multiple fronts. She found her passion for creative writing at a young age and honed her skills throughout college while she obtained a BA in Communication Studies.

Since graduating from the University of North Texas, Hannah resides in Dallas with her Keeshond pup, Pepper, her partner, Sergio, and his Alaskan Malamute, Kodiak. She enjoys fostering for local shelters and rescues, giving a home to those in need while in search of their furever home. Connect with Hannah on Instagram @hannah.mosing.

Milton Keynes UK
Ingram Content Group UK Ltd.
UKHW031016200324
439740UK00018B/192/J